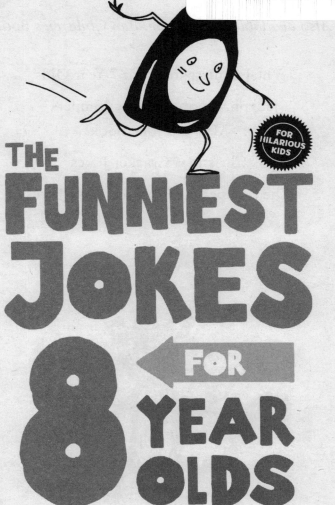

THE FUNNIEST JOKES

JOKES

8

FOR

YEAR

OLDS

THE FUNNIEST JOKES

FOR HILARIOUS KIDS

JOKES

8 FOR YEAR OLDS

Compiled by Amanda Li

Illustrated by Jane Eccles

MACMILLAN CHILDREN'S BOOKS

Published 2021 by Macmillan Children's Books
an imprint of Pan Macmillan
The Smithson, 6 Briset Street, London EC1M 5NR
EU representative: Macmillan Publishers Ireland Limited,
Mallard Lodge, Lansdowne Village, Dublin 4
Associated companies throughout the world
www.panmacmillan.com

ISBN 978-1-5290-6599-2

1 3 5 7 9 8 6 4 2

A CIP catalogue record for this book is available from the British Library.

Printed and bound by CPI Group (UK) Ltd, Croydon CR0 4YY
Compiled by Amanda Li
Design by Perfect Bound Ltd

MIX
Paper from
responsible sources
FSC® C116313
FSC
www.fsc.org

Why do people avoid
dinosaurs?
Because their eggs stink.

What do you call baby
dinosaurs?
Triceratots.

1

What do you get when
you cross a hedgehog
with a balloon?

POP!

Why are seagulls found
by the sea?

**Because if they lived
by the bay, they'd be
bagels.**

Why is the letter 'T' important
to a stick insect?

**Because without it,
it would be a sick insect.**

Why can't horses play
football?

**Because they've
got two left feet.**

Boy: Dad, did you get
a haircut?

Dad: No, I got them all cut.

What do sheep do
after Christmas?

**They write
thank ewe letters.**

Millie: What's 5Q plus 5Q?
Tilly: Ten Q.
Millie: You're welcome!

What do monsters write at the end of their messages?

Beast wishes.

What do skeletons sell at school fairs?

Rattle tickets.

Where do you take a
sick wasp?

To the waspital.

Knock, knock!

Who's there?

Ben.

Ben who?

**Ben knocking on this
door for ages!**

Where do fishermen
go on holiday?

Any plaice will do.

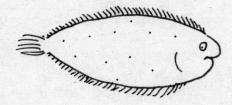

What bird is always out
of breath?

A puffin.

Why did the girl take a
ladder to school?

**She was going to
high school.**

What does a baby witch
call her broomstick?

A broom broom.

What do you call a monster
with no neck?

The Lost Neck monster.

Why are cats bad storytellers?

**Because they only have
one tale.**

What do you call a friend
who's just been squashed
by an elephant?

A flatmate.

Knock, knock!
Who's there?
Luke.
Luke who?
Luke out, there's a monster behind you!

What do you call a man
with a spade?

Doug.

What do you call a man
with a plank on his head?

Edward.

What do you call a man
with a wig on his head?

Aaron.

What do you call a man on
your front doorstep?

Matt.

Patient: Doctor, doctor!
I keep thinking I'm a crocodile.
Doctor: Snap out of it!

Patient: Doctor, doctor!
I keep thinking I'm a
strawberry.
Doctor: Well, you are
in a jam!

Why did the porcupine
shout 'OW, OW, OW!'

**He put his coat on
inside out.**

OW!

Where do you find a tortoise with no legs?

Where you left it.

How do you tell the difference between tinned beans and tinned custard?

Read the labels.

What stands in the
middle of Paris?
The letter 'R'.

Knock, knock!
Who's there?
Kanga.
Kanga who?
No, kangaROO!

What do you call a man
who can't stand?

Neil.

What do you call a
man with a seagull
on his head?

Cliff.

What do you call a man
in the middle of the sea?

Bob.

Why did the centipede
miss the train?

**He had to stop and
tie his shoelaces.**

Where do ghosts go
on holiday?

The Isle of Fright.

Patient: Doctor, doctor! My eyesight is getting worse.

Person: You're right, this is the post office!

Patient: Doctor, doctor! I keep thinking I'm a spoon.

Doctor: Just sit down and don't stir!

What do you get if you cross a frog with a traffic warden?

Toad away.

What do you call a sheep
covered in chocolate?

A candy baa.

Why don't pirates know
their alphabet properly?

**Because they think
there are seven 'C's!**

If I cut a potato in two,
I have two halves.
If I cut a potato in four,
I have four quarters.
What do I get if I cut a potato
in sixteen?

Chips.

Where do spiders play
football?

At Webley Stadium.

Why was the mummy
glow-worm sad?

**Her children weren't
very bright.**

What kind of music
do rabbits listen to?

Hip hop.

How do you communicate with
aliens in deep space?

Shout very loudly.

What did the dragon say when
he met a knight in armour?

'Ooh, I love
tinned food!'

What do you call a man
in a pile of leaves?

Russell.

What do you call a man
who loves exploring?

Seymour.

Where do astronauts
keep their sandwiches?

In a launch box.

How do you know if there's an
alien in your house?

**There's a spaceship
parked in your garden.**

What did one fire say to
the other fire?

**'Let's go out
together!'**

What do you call a play
acted by ghosts?

A phantomime.

How do you contact an alien
who lives on Saturn?

Give it a ring.

Did you hear the joke
about the rope?

Let's skip it.

What do you get
when a giant ape does
martial arts?

King Kong-fu.

Knock, knock!
Who's there?
Aladdin.
Aladdin who?
Aladdin the street wants to play with you!

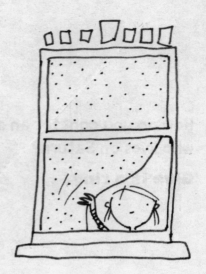

What do astronauts drink at breaktimes?
Gravi-tea.

How do monkeys get
down the stairs?

**They slide down the
banana-ster.**

What did the ghost
eat for dinner?

Spook-hetti.

What's big, grey and
stinky?

A smellyphant.

What would you do if an
elephant sat in front of
you at the movies?

Miss most of the film.

What kind of elephants
live in the Arctic?

Cold ones.

What's big, grey and
goes up and down?

**An elephant on a
trampoline.**

How do we know carrots are
good for your eyesight?

**Well, have you ever
seen a rabbit
wearing glasses?**

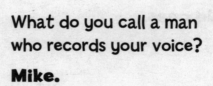

What do you call a man
who records your voice?

Mike.

What do you call a man
who steals your money?

Rob.

Millie: A cat just scratched my leg.

Tilly: I'll put some cream on it.

Millie: But it'll be miles away by now!

Why do mummies go on holiday?

To relax and unwind.

What's the coldest
place in the world?

Chile.

Where do aliens leave
their spaceships?

**At parking
meteors.**

What happened when a
woman landed in a vat
of curry?

She fell into a korma.

What do you call a
man with a rabbit up
his jumper?

Warren.

What do you get if a
naughty rabbit sits on
your head?

A bad hare day.

What did the pig say
on a hot day?

'I'm bacon!'

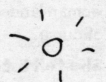

What do Alexander the
Great and Winnie-the-Pooh
have in common?

The same middle name.

Which athlete stays
warm in the winter?

A long jumper.

Knock, knock!
Who's there?
Nose.
Nose who?
**Nose a lot of
jokes, I do!**

What word is always spelt
incorrectly?

Incorrectly.

Patient: Doctor, doctor!
I keep thinking I'm a sheep.
Doctor: How are you feeling?
Patient: Baaa-d! Really Baaa-d!

Why should you never eat lunch
with basketball players?

Because they dribble all the time.

Patient: Doctor, doctor! I keep thinking I'm a dustbin.

Doctor: Oh, stop talking rubbish!

What do you call a teacher who's always late?

Mister Bus.

Who invented King Arthur's round table?

Sir Cumference.

Why did the one-eyed monster have to close his school?

Because he only had one pupil.

How do you throw a party in space?

Plan-et.

What do knights do when they
are scared of the dark?

Turn on a knight light.

What's a knight's favourite fish?

A swordfish.

What do you call two elephants at the pool?

A pair of swimming trunks.

Why are elephants so wrinkly?

Well, have you ever tried ironing one?

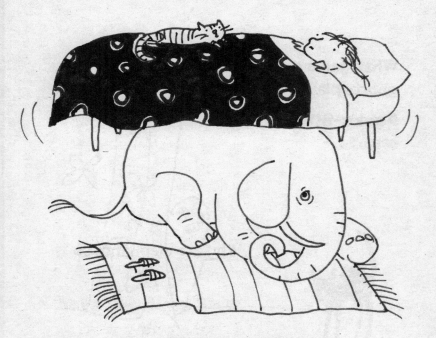

How can you tell when there's an elephant under your bed?

When you're almost touching the ceiling.

What's the difference between a banana and an elephant?

You can't peel an elephant?

What game do baby
ghosts play?

Peeka-BOO!

What's red and invisible?

No tomatoes.

Why should you never share
a bed with a pig?

They hog the duvet.

What did the bumble bee
football player say?

'Hive scored!'

Knock, knock!

Who's there?

Waiter.

Waiter who?

**Waiter minute while
I tie my shoelaces!**

What do you get if you cross a skunk with a hot-air balloon?

Something that stinks to high heaven.

What did the short-sighted hedgehog say to the cactus?

'Oh, there you are, Mum!'

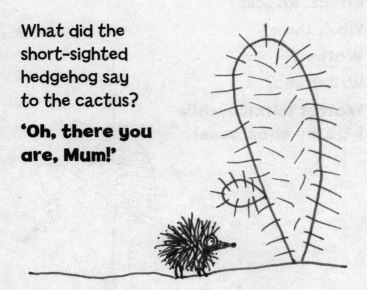

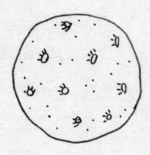

Where do aliens go to study?

Mooniversity.

Why did the boy go to bed in the fireplace?

He wanted to sleep like a log.

What do you get if you cross a chicken with a dog?

Pooched eggs.

Why are witches such
good writers?

**Because they
are great at
spelling.**

Where do you take
a frog with bad
eyesight?

To the hoptician.

What kind of lion never roars?

A dandelion.

What goes 'Trot-dash,
trot-trot-dash?'

Horse code.

What's the fastest vegetable?

A runner bean.

What did the earwig sing at the football match?

'Earwig go, earwig go, earwig go!'

Millie: I went riding yesterday.

Tilly: Horseback?

Millie: Yes, it got back two hours before me!

Why couldn't cave people send Christmas cards?

Because the stamps wouldn't stick to the rocks.

Patient: Doctor, doctor! I only have fifty-nine seconds to live.

Doctor: Hang on, I'll be with you in a minute!

Patient: Doctor, doctor! I think I've swallowed a clock.

Doctor: There's no need for alarm!

What do you say
to a frog who
wants a lift?

'Hop in!'

Why did the beekeeper give
away his bees?

They were free bees.

Where did the monster go when
he lost his hand?

To the second-hand shop.

How did the witch know she
was getting better?

**Because the doctor let
her out of bed for a spell.**

What kind of noise
annoys an oyster?

**A noisy noise annoys
an oyster.**

What does it mean if you find
a horseshoe?

**That somewhere a horse
is walking around in his
socks.**

Why did the horse cross the road?

Because someone shouted 'Hey!'

Why are 'A's like
flowers?

**Because 'B's come
after them.**

What did one candle say to
another candle?

'Are you going out tonight?'

What should you say if
you meet a toad?

'Warts new?'

What must you never
do in a submarine?

**Open a window for
fresh air.**

Knock, knock!

Who's there?

Ketchup.

Ketchup who?

Ketchup with me if you can!

What do you get if
you cross a dinosaur
with a pig?

Jurassic Pork.

What time do ducks get up?

At the quack of dawn.

What did the fish say
after it was pulled out
of the water?

'Long time, no sea!'

What did the mummy
bee say to the naughty
baby bee?

'Beehive yourself!'

What did the fish finger
say to the tomato?

**'That's enough of
your sauce!'**

What instrument can
a fisherman play?

The cast-a-net.

Why did the musician
get locked out?

**He'd got the
wrong key.**

What do you call a rabbit
with no clothes on?

A bare hare.

What cheese is made
back to front?

Edam.

Patient: Doctor, doctor! I think I'm invisible.

Doctor: I'm sorry - I can't see you right now!

Why did the doctor take his nose to pieces?

He wanted to see what made it run.

What board game do aliens play?

Moon-opoly.

Did you hear the joke about the pizza?

Never mind, it's too cheesey.

Why wasn't the vampire
invited to the party?

**Because he was a pain
in the neck.**

What do you call an
exploding monkey?

A ba-boom!

Why don't lions like fast food?

**Because they can't
catch it.**

How do trees get online?

They just log on.

What's brown and sticky?

A stick.

Knock, knock!
Who's there?
Nanna.
Nanna who?
Nanna your business!

What trees do ghosts
like best?

Ceme-trees.

What should you do if you find a monster in the shower?

Wait until he's finished.

What did the duck say to the waiter?

'Put it on my bill, please!'

How do you make
a fool laugh on
Christmas Day?

**Tell him a joke on
Christmas Eve.**

What did Adam say to his
girlfriend the day before
Christmas?

'It's Christmas, Eve!'

What do you get if you cross Father Christmas with a detective?

Santa Clues.

What illness can you catch at Christmas?

Tinsel-itus.

What goes 'Now you see me,
now you don't, now you see me,
now you don't?'

**A snowman on a zebra
crossing.**

What did Santa
Claus say to Mrs
Santa Claus?

**'It looks like
rain, dear!'**

What's green, covered in
tinsel and goes 'Croak!'

A mistle-toad.

Where do snowmen
go to dance?

Snowballs.

What do sharks read
before they go to sleep?

A bite-time story.

What did one flea say to
another flea?

'Shall we walk or catch a dog?'

What treatment do you
give a sick lemon?

Lemon-aid.

What can a whole
orange do that half
an orange can't?

Look round.

Why does a monkey scratch itself?

Because he's the only one who knows where it itches.

Knock, knock!
Who's there?
Elsie.
Elsie who?
Elsie you later!

What's small, cuddly and bright red?

A koala bear holding its breath.

Why do koala bears study hard?

For the koalafications.

What's worse than finding a slug in your sandwich?

Finding half a slug.

What do you call
a monster in a
telephone box?

Stuck.

How can you tell the oldest
rabbits in a group?

**Look for the grey
hares.**

What's black and white
and blue?

A freezing-cold zebra.

What do you get if you cross a cow with an old map?

Udderly lost.

Why did the boy throw his toast out of the window?

He wanted to see the butterfly.

What's the difference between a piano and a fish?

You can tune a piano but you can't tunafish.

Why do bananas always use sunscreen?

Because they peel easily.

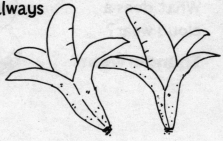

Why do birds fly?

Because it's faster than walking.

What did one mushroom say to another mushroom?

'You're a fun guy!'

What does a
cloud wear?

Thunderwear.

What did one traffic light say
to another traffic light?

'Don't look, I'm changing!'

Where do sharks
go on summer
holidays?

Finland.

What's the quietest sport?

**Bowling - you can hear
a pin drop.**

Why is a tennis game
very noisy?

**Because the
players raise a
racket.**

How do you know if a baby
skeleton is in the room?

You can hear its rattle.

What did the skeleton
eat at the barbecue?

Spare ribs.

What do skeletons say before dinner?

'Bone appetit!'

Why are ghosts bad at telling lies?

Because you can see right through them.

Why are ghosts good at team games?

Because of their team spirit.

How long does it take to
learn to ice skate?

A few sittings.

How does Jack Frost
get to work?

By icicle.

What should you never
eat before breakfast?

Lunch and dinner.

Why was the apple pie
out of breath?

**It was made from
puff pastry.**

How do
you make
a sausage roll?

Push it down a hill.

How do you stop a
bull from charging?

Unplug its phone.

What did the dog say
to the bone?

**'Nice gnawing
you!'**

Which monster is extremely
untidy?

The Loch Mess monster.

What did the dog say
when it sat on some
sandpaper?

'Ruff!'

What did one slug say
to another?

'See you next slime!'

Why do hamsters like
spinning on wheels?

Because it's wheely fun.

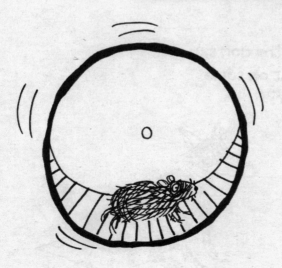

Why can't a bicycle
stand up?

It's too tyred.

Who invented fire?

Some bright spark.

Knock, knock!
Who's there?
Hatch.
Hatch who?
Bless you!

When is a swimming
costume like a bell?

When you wring it out.

Why do penguins carry fish
in their beaks?

**Because they haven't
got any pockets.**

What do you get if you
cross a bear with a skunk?

Winnie-the-Pooh.

What did one calculator say
to the other calculator?

'You can count on me!'

What's a snake's favourite
football team?

Slitherpool.

What did one pencil
say to the other pencil?

'You have a good point!'

Knock, knock!
Who's there?
Arthur.
Arthur who?
**Arthur any more
biscuits in the tin?**

How do monkeys
make toast?

Put it under a gorilla.

What did the right eye say
to the left eye?

**'Between you and me, there's
something that smells!'**

What did the hungry
clock do?

**It went back four
seconds.**

What do rabbits use to
keep their fur tidy?

Hare-spray.

Why do bees hum?

Because they don't know the words.

What do you get if you cross a snake with a magician?

Abra-da-cobra.

How do electric eels taste?

Shocking.

What animal does everyone
look like in the shower?

A little bear.

What did one volcano
say to another?

'I lava you!'

How do you find out
the price of a sheep?

Scan its baa-code.

Why do oysters never
share their pearls?

**Because they're
shellfish.**

What do you call a
monkey that loves chips?

A chipmonk.

Why do dragons sleep during
the day?

**So that they can fight
knights.**

Did I ever tell you the joke
about the roof?

It's way over your head.

What did one library book
say to another?

'Can I take you out?'

Why did the thief keep his
money in a freezer?

He wanted cold, hard cash.

What do you call a camel
with three humps?

Humphrey.

What's the difference between an alligator and a post box?

If you don't know, be careful next time you post a letter.

What do you get when you cross a dinosaur with a firework?

Dino-mite.

Why did the computer squeak?

Somebody stepped on its mouse.

Did you hear about the
restaurant on the moon?

It had no atmosphere.

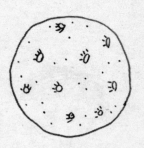

What kind of tiles can't
be stuck on walls?

Reptiles.

What do you get
when you cross a
snake and a pie?

A python.

What did the pony say
when he coughed?

**'Excuse me,
I'm a little hoarse!'**

What do you call a Roman emperor with a cold?

Julius Sneezer.

Knock, knock!
Who's there?
Felix.
Felix who?
**Felix my ice cream,
I'll lick his!**

What did the worst athlete in the world do?

Ran a bath and came in second.

On what day do
monsters eat people?

Chews-day.

How does a monster greet a human?

'Pleased to eat you!'

How do you feel about a cat eating breakfast with a spoon?

It's pretty impawsible.

What did one plate say to another plate?

'Dinner's on me!'

Did you hear the one about the butter?

Actually, I don't want to spread it around.

Why do dogs run in circles?

Because they can't run in squares.

What's pink and cuts the grass?

A prawnmower.

What kind of beans do monsters eat?

Human beans.

What do wolves do during the summer?

Go on howliday.

What kind of training does a rubbish collector need?

None - you just pick it up as you go along.

When does a pirate
get a new ship?

When it's on sail.

Where did Napoleon
keep his armies?

Up his sleevies.

What's an ig?

**An igloo without
a loo.**

Why was the broom
running late?

It over-swept.

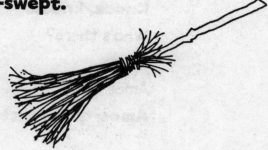

Why did the golfer
have an extra pair
of socks?

**In case he got a
hole in one.**

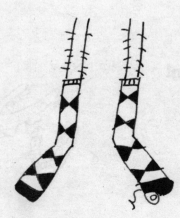

Knock, knock!
Who's there?
Amos.
Amos who?
Amos-quito just bit me!

Knock, knock!
Who's there?
Andy.
Andy who?
Andy bit me again!

What goes 'Oh, oh, oh!'

Santa Claus walking backwards.

What's brown and creeps around at Christmas?

A mince spy.

When is a car not a car?

When it turns into a garage.

What should you do if a dog eats your pencil?

Use a pen instead.

When is a door
not a door?

When it's ajar.

Why did the boy put salad
dressing in his bed?

He wanted to wake up oily.

What do you get if you cross
a pie and a rat?

A pirate.

What's the biggest kind of ant?

A giant.

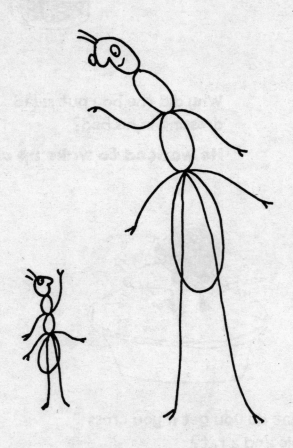

What did the grape say
when it got squashed?

**Nothing. It let out
a little whine.**

Knock, knock!
Who's there?
Spell.
Spell who?
OK - W-H-O!

Which pet is always smiling?

A grinny pig.

What kind of pet lies around
on the floor all day?

A carpet.

What do snakes have on
the front of their cars?

Windscreen vipers.

Which insects live in
haunted houses?

Eerie wigs.

What did the frog say
at the party?

**'Time's fun when
you're having flies!'**

What steps should you
take if a tiger is running
towards you?

Really big ones.

Why can't you play a joke
on a snake?

**Because you can never
pull its leg.**

Knock, knock!
Who's there?
Water.
Water who?
**Water you doing?
Just open the door!**

Where do baby apes sleep?

Apricots.

What does a caterpillar sleep on?

A caterpillow.

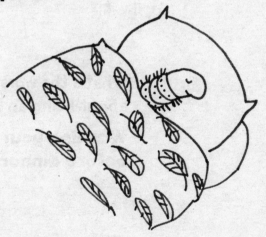

How do you pay an octopus?

Just give him a few squid.

What's the worst thing
about being an octopus?

**Washing your hands
before dinner.**

What's big, grey and stops
you from getting wet?

An umbrellaphant.

What should you take if you go bungee jumping with an elephant?

Very strong elastic.

What should you do if you find an elephant in your bed?

Sleep on the sofa.

What do dogs eat
at the cinema?

Pupcorn.

Why can't dogs work the
DVD remote?

**Because they always
hit the paws button.**

Dan: I've been on my computer all night.

Stan: I've been on my bed – it's more comfortable!

What's the last thing you take off when you go to bed?

Your feet off the floor.

What do you call a sleeping bull?

A bulldozer.

Two flies were playing football in a saucer.

One said, 'We need to train hard – we're playing in the cup next week!'

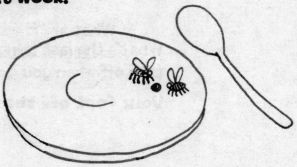

What did the goalkeeper have for lunch?

Beans on post.

What do you call a fly with no wings?

A walk.

What did the gymnast
have for lunch?

A few rolls.

What are the strongest
creatures in the ocean?

Mussels.

Who's in goal when the ghost
team plays football?

The ghoulie, of course.